WASHINGTON

Laura Pratt

Go to **www.av2books.com**, and enter this book's unique code.

BOOK CODE

C443481

AV² by Weigl brings you media enhanced books that support active learning.

AV² provides enriched content that supplements and complements this book. Weigl's AV² books strive to create inspired learning and engage young minds in a total learning experience.

Your AV² Media Enhanced books come alive with...

Audio
Listen to sections of the book read aloud.

Video
Watch informative video clips.

Embedded Weblinks
Gain additional information for research.

Try This!
Complete activities and hands-on experiments.

Key Words
Study vocabulary, and complete a matching word activity.

Quizzes
Test your knowledge.

Slide Show
View images and captions, and prepare a presentation.

... and much, much more!

Published by AV² by Weigl
350 5th Avenue, 59th Floor
New York, NY 10118
Website: www.av2books.com   www.weigl.com

Library of Congress Cataloging-in-Publication Data
Pratt, Laura.
 Washington / by Laura Pratt.
   p. cm. -- (Explore the U.S.A.)
 Includes bibliographical references and index.
 ISBN 978-1-61913-415-7 (hard cover : alk. paper)
 1. Washington (State)--Juvenile literature. I. Title.
 F891.3.P73 2012
 976.8--dc23
                        2012016586

Printed in the United States of America in North Mankato, Minnesota
1 2 3 4 5 6 7 8 9   16 15 14 13 12

052012
WEP040512

Project Coordinator: Karen Durrie
Art Director: Terry Paulhus

Weigl acknowledges Getty Images as the primary image supplier for this title.

WASHINGTON

Contents

2 AV² Book Code
4 Nickname
6 Location
8 History
10 Flower and Seal
12 Flag
14 Animal
16 Capital
18 Goods
20 Fun Things to Do
22 Facts
24 Key Words

3

This is Washington.
It is called the Evergreen State.
Washington has many forests.

This is the shape of Washington. It is in the north part of the United States. Two states and Canada border Washington.

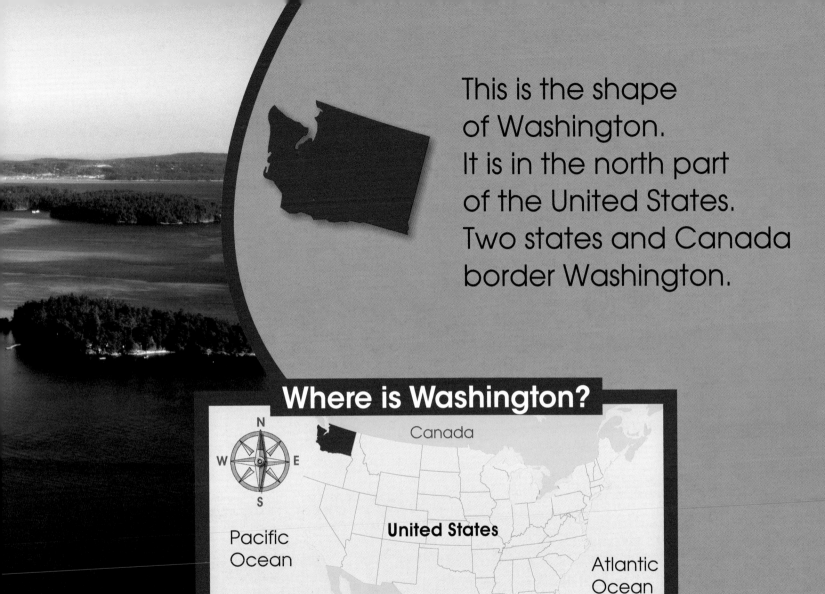

Where is Washington?

Canada

Pacific Ocean

United States

Atlantic Ocean

Mexico

Washington is next to the Pacific Ocean.

The city of Seattle had the World's Fair in 1962. A tower called the Space Needle was built for the fair.

More than two million people visited the Space Needle during the World's Fair.

The coast rhododendron is the Washington state flower. It grows on shrubs.

The Washington state seal shows President George Washington.

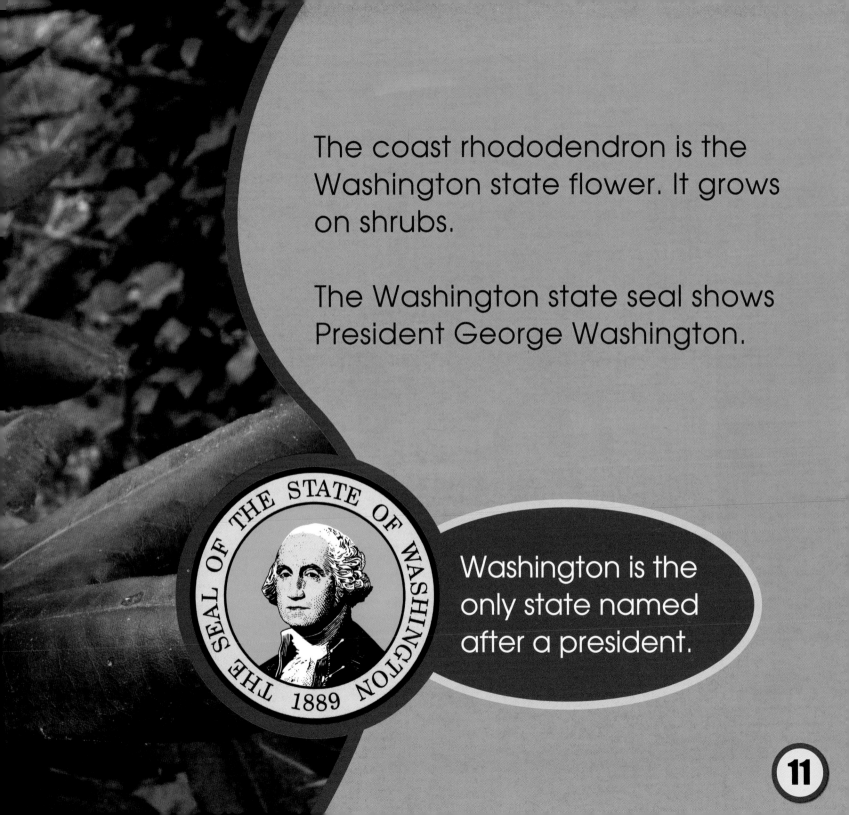

THE SEAL OF THE STATE OF WASHINGTON
1889

Washington is the only state named after a president.

This is the state flag of Washington. It is green with the state seal in the middle.

The Washington flag is the only state flag that shows a historic person.

The orca is the Washington state marine animal. Orcas are a part of the dolphin family. They live in groups called pods.

An orca can be up to 32 feet long.

This city is named Olympia. It is the Washington state capital.

American Indians have lived near Olympia for at least 12,000 years.

Apples grow in Washington. Washington grows more apples than any other state.

About 12 billion apples are hand picked in Washington each year.

Washington is known for its beautiful mountains, coastline, and islands.

People can take a ferry to the San Juan Islands to explore beaches and watch whales.

21

WASHINGTON FACTS

These pages provide detailed information that expands on the interesting facts found in the book. These pages are intended to be used by adults as a learning support to help young readers round out their knowledge of each state in the *Explore the U.S.A.* series.

Pages 4–5

Washington has many forests with evergreen trees such as fir and pine. About 21 million acres (8.5 million hectares) of Washington are forested. The highest point in Washington is Mount Rainier. It is 14,400 feet (4,400 meters) tall. There are two volcanoes at its peak.

Pages 6–7

On November 11, 1889, Washington became the 42nd state to join the United States. Washington is in an area known as the Pacific Northwest. Some parts of Washington are among the rainiest places in the world. Washington has lakes, mountains, glaciers, volcanoes, deserts, and rainforests.

Pages 8–9

The World's Fair is an international exposition that features displays from many countries from around the world. The theme of the 1962 Seattle World's Fair was "the space age." Many futuristic structures were built in Seattle, including the Space Needle and a monorail train system. The Space Needle is 605 feet (184 meters) tall and has a revolving restaurant. About 10 million people visited the fair.

Pages 10–11

Washington women voted the coast rhododendron the state flower in 1892. They wanted to find a flower that they could enter in a floral exhibit at the next World's Fair. The state seal features the first president of the United States. The portrait of George Washington was made by an artist named Gilbert Stuart.

Pages 12–13

The Washington flag was adopted in 1923. It is the only state flag with a green background. Washington was a state for more than 30 years before it had an official flag. The Washington flag may be fringed in the same shade of gold found on the seal.

Pages 14–15

About 88 orcas live in the waters of Washington's Puget Sound. The number of orcas in Washington has been declining due to human activity, reduction of food sources, pollution, and other changes to the ocean environment. Orcas are the largest member of the dolphin family. They can weigh up to 6 tons (5.4 tonnes).

Pages 16–17

Olympia is a small city of about 46,000 people. It is located on the southern point of Puget Sound. American Indians had lived in Washington long before European settlers arrived. American Indians in the area included the Makah, Quinalt, and Snohomish on the coast, and the Spokane, Yakama, and Nez Perce in the east.

Pages 18–19

There are about 175,000 acres (71 ha) of apple orchards in the Cascade Mountains of Washington. Many kinds of apples are grown there, including Red and Golden Delicious, Braeburn, and Honeycrisp. More than 100 million 40-pound (18-kilogram) boxes of apples are harvested in Washington each year.

Pages 20–21

Washington's San Juan Islands is an archipelago made up of 172 islands. Ferry boats serve the four largest islands. These islands are Shaw Island, Lopez Island, Orcas Island, and San Juan Island. The islands have forests, mountains, and beaches. Many tourists visit the San Juan Islands each year to see orca, minke, and gray whales.

KEY WORDS

Research has shown that as much as 65 percent of all written material published in English is made up of 300 words. These 300 words cannot be taught using pictures or learned by sounding them out. They must be recognized by sight. This book contains 59 common sight words to help young readers improve their reading fluency and comprehension. This book also teaches young readers several important content words, such as proper nouns. These words are paired with pictures to aid in learning and improve understanding.

Page	Sight Words First Appearance
5	has, is, it, many, state, the, this
7	and, of, in, next, part, to, two, where
8	city, for, had, more, people, than, was, world's
11	a, after, grows, named, on, only, shows
12	that, with
15	an, animal, are, be, can, family, feet, groups, live, long, they, up
16	at, American, have, Indians, near, years
19	about, any, each, hand, other
21	its, mountains, take, watch

Page	Content Words First Appearance
5	forests, Washington
7	Canada, Pacific Ocean, shape, United States
8	fair, Seattle, Space Needle, tower
11	coast rhododendron, flower, George Washington, president, shrubs, seal
12	flag, middle, person
15	orca, pods
16	capital, Olympia
19	apples
21	beaches, coastline, ferry, islands, San Juan, whales

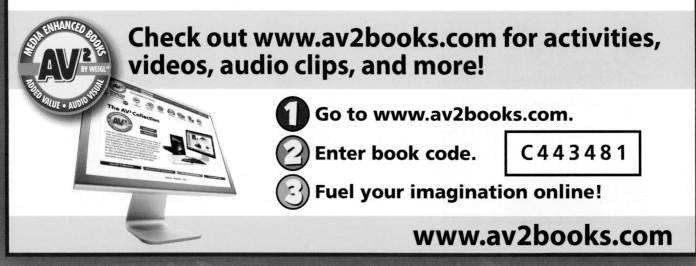

Check out www.av2books.com for activities, videos, audio clips, and more!

1 Go to www.av2books.com.

2 Enter book code. C443481

3 Fuel your imagination online!

www.av2books.com